A CHAMPION'S Heart

Written by **Brian Mitchell**

Illustrations by **Sharon Jones-Scaife**

A CHAMPION'S HEART
PUBLISHED BY FROG POND PUBLISHING
P.O. Box 452721
Garland, TX 75045-2721
Paperback ISBN-13: 978-1-7368929-0-9
ISBN-10: 1-7368929-0-8

Copyright © 2019 by Brian Mitchell
Illustrations © 2019 by Sharon Jones-Scaife

All rights reserved. No part of this book may be reproduced or transmitted in any form or by any means, electronic or mechanical, including photocopying and recording, or by any information storage and retrieval system without permission in writing from the publisher.

Edited by Ann Fields & Wendy Stewart
Published in the United States by Coffee Creek Media Group.

To my parents
Blanche Mitchell, Sr. and Sophonia Mitchell

Thank you for believing in me, for inspiring me,
for loving me, for leading me and encouraging me
to be the best person I can be. Without your love and
selfless commitment to our family, nothing that I have
accomplished would have been possible.

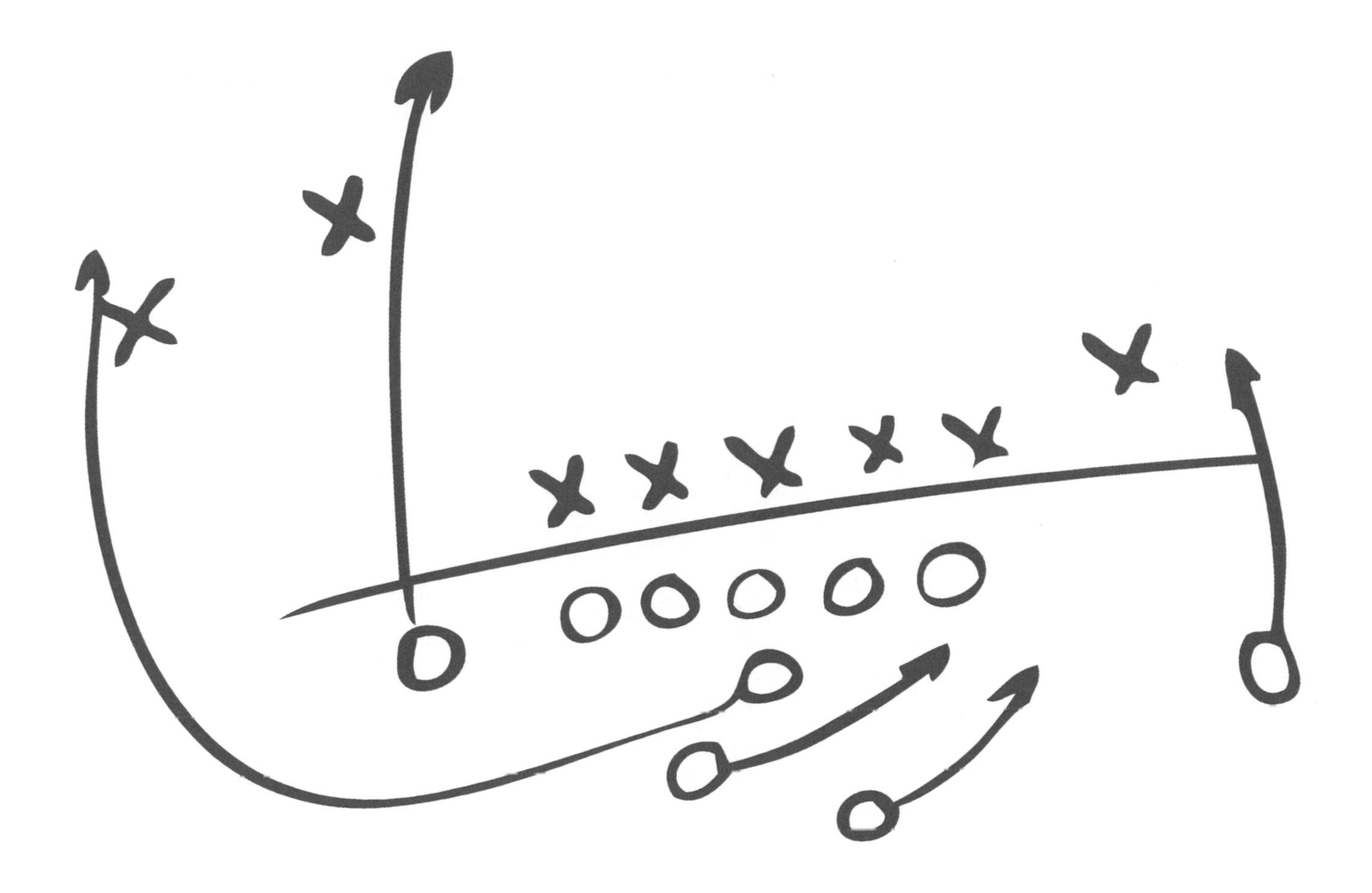

Playing football in the National Football League **had always been my dream.** My love for the game started at a very early age, which means my work to be one of the **greatest punt return specialist in the NFL** started at a very early age.

Growing up in **Plaquemine, Louisiana,** I was the youngest of seven kids and one of the smallest in my neighborhood. I began playing football, competing with and against my brothers, cousins, and neighborhood friends, but their ages and bigger sizes didn't deter me.

I stayed with **football** because **I loved its competitive nature.** Also, I was **good** at it, and I felt it could **provide** an opportunity to get a college education.

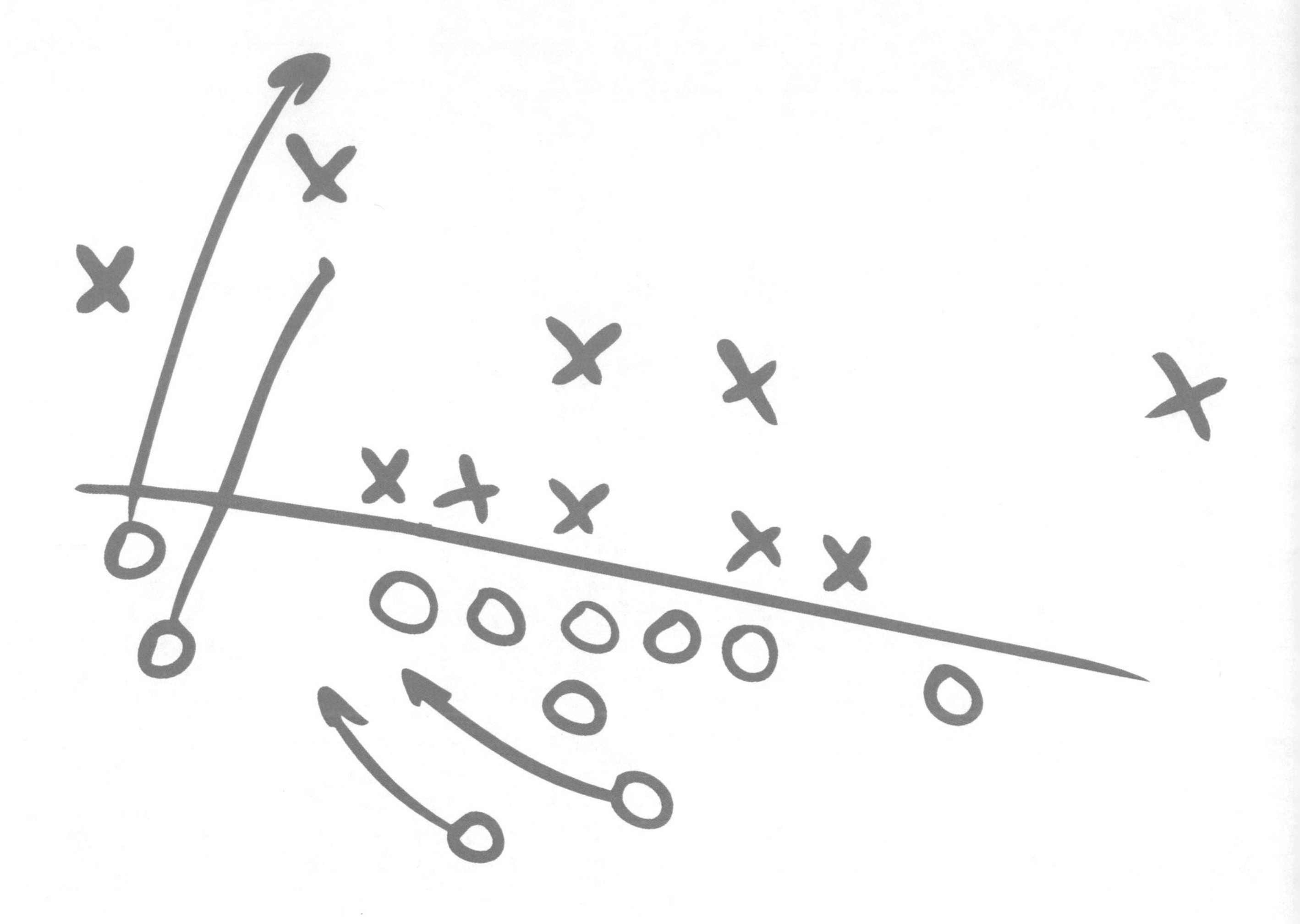

First Down

My parents always made sure **education was my top priority. Football came second.** I was very fortunate to have both my father and mother in the home. I felt rich growing up because **my parents invested so much love** and **care** into me.

A+
Brian
A+
Brian

I was blessed to have other **role models,** too - **my sisters, Linda** and **Freda; my brother, Daryl;** and **teachers, Mrs. Carolyn Brown** and **Mrs. Marilyn Brown.** They, along with my parents, **poured into my life.** They encouraged me, challenged me, and convinced me **I could accomplish whatever I set out to do.** They **instilled confidence,** and told me **there were no limits in my life.**

I **listened** to my parents, siblings, and teachers, and **worked as hard in the classroom** as I worked **on the field because I did not want to disappoint them.**

The winning play: Show **appreciation** to your family for the **time and money** they invest in you. **Choose role** models who will have a **positive impact on your life** and who you don't want to disappoint.

#12

I was **confident** that I would be **successful at whatever I set out to be** because my father told me in fifth grade that **I was a Mitchell** and that **I could do anything.** Knowing that early on **set the tone for the rest of my life.** I have always **believed in myself.**

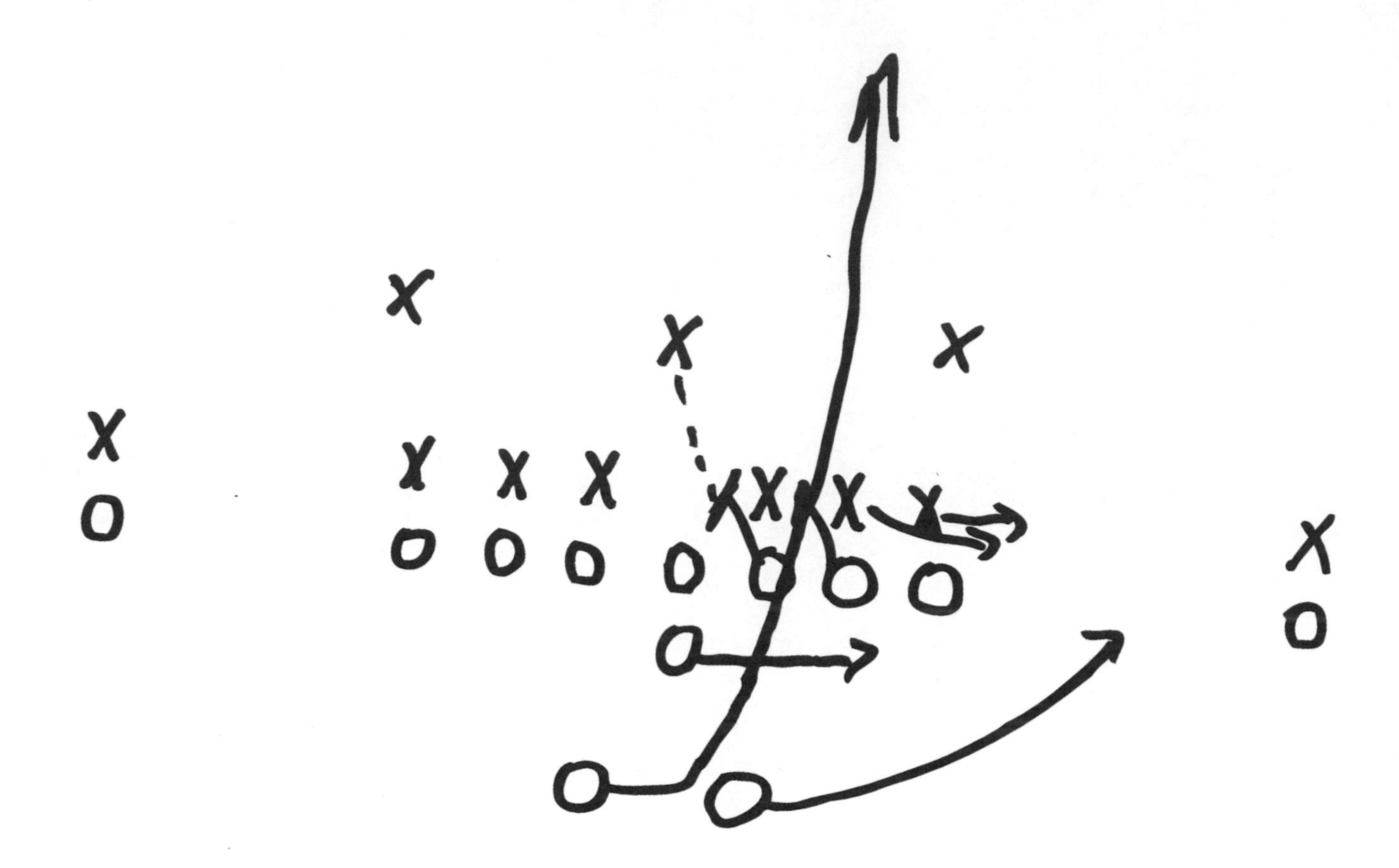

Second Down

My decision to attend the **University of Southwestern Louisiana** was one of the **best decisions I've made.** I was allowed to **focus** on both my **academic career** in **Engineering** and to **play football.**

RAGIN' CAJUNS

CAJUNS
1

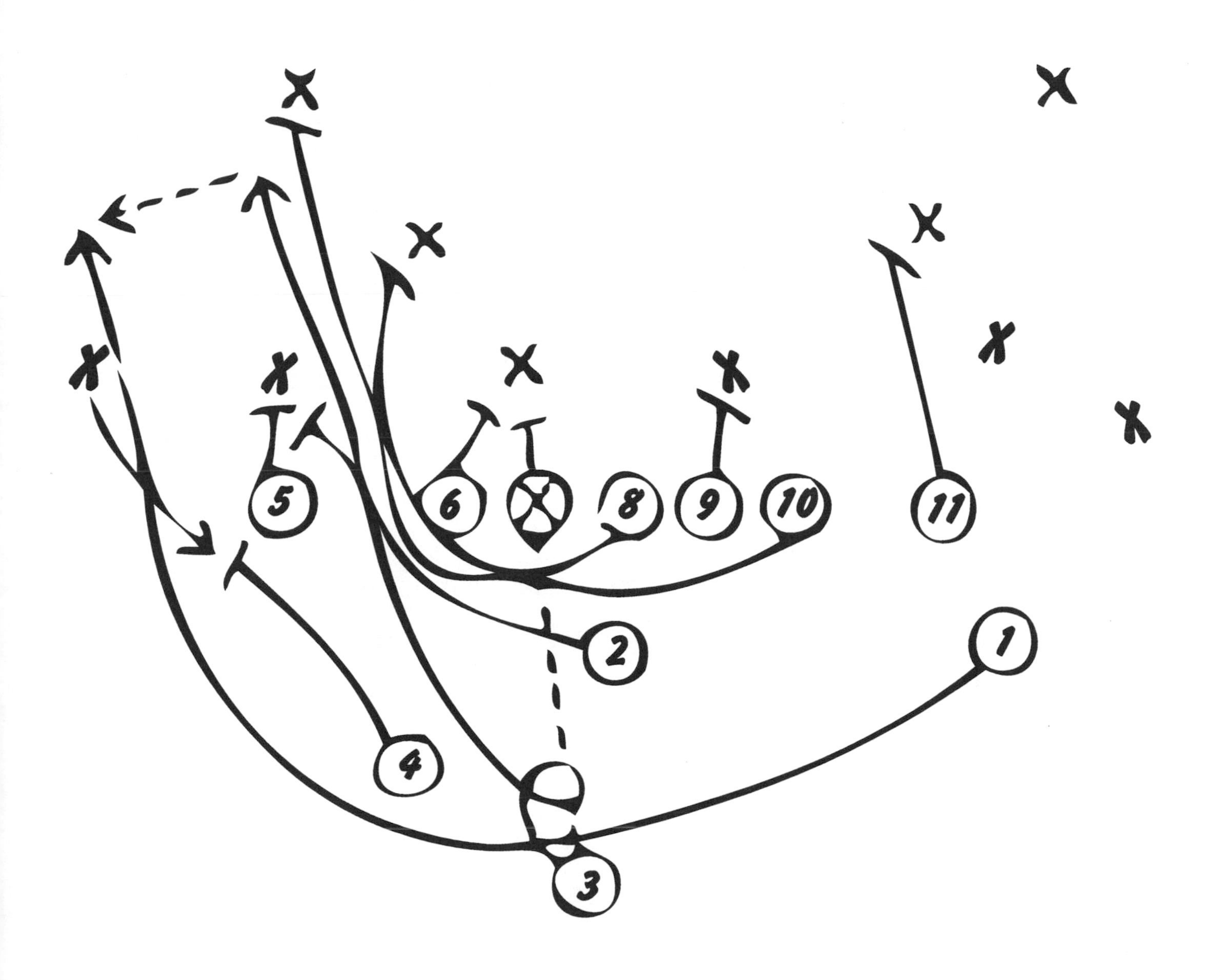

I started my college career sharing the quarterback role with another player, and midway through my **sophomore year, I earned** the starting position at **quarterback.** This accomplishment came with a lot of pressure. Not only was I adjusting to a **tough academic workload,** but also I was **learning my team and my coaches,** adjusting to a **faster paced game,** and working to **earn the trust** of my older teammates.

During my college athletic career, I set many football records. I was the **first player in NCAA** history to **pass for more than 5,000 yards** (5,447) and **rush for more than 3,000 yards** (3,335). I also held the NCAA record for **most rushing touchdowns by a quarterback** (47). As a senior, **I rushed for 1,311 yards** and **passed for 1,993 yards** while accounting for **25 touchdowns** (six passing, 19 rushing).

In the classroom and on the football field, I never went out to set any records or receive accolades. I simply went out each day to **better myself** and **improve at the game. I never let outside influences affect my own personal goals.** My goals and desire were to **work hard** and **be successful.**

The winning play: Think long and hard about decisions. Every **decision** you make, on and off the field, will have an **impact in your life.** Stay **focused** on both dreams – education and sports – and **work hard** in both areas.

UNIVERSITY OF SOUTHWESTERN LOUISIANA

Third Down

On **April 23, 1990,** I was selected in the fifth round **(130th overall)** of the **NFL draft** by **Washington.** This was the day I had **dreamed** of. The minute I received the call and heard my name – **Brian Mitchell** and **Washington** -- I knew all of my **hard work** and **determination** had paid off.

Although **I had worked hard all of my life** to get to the NFL, I realized I was going to have to **work even harder** to be **successful** at the p**rofessional level.** I did not just want to be on the team, I wanted to **be the best player I could be!**

My goal was to be in the NFL in any capacity, not just as a quarterback. When I got the opportunity, I started to **study the game and the role** that I accepted. My first NFL return was a touchdown. At that point and for the next 14 years, my mindset was to **be the first there** and **the last to leave.** No one was going to outwork me. I was **determined to get better** and better.

We all have a point where we think we **can't go any further or get any better,** but growing up with a military father, I was constantly told **"there's always room to grow and get better, there's always limits to exceed." The underlying message** from him was to **always do the work** and **keep working hard.** He reminded me to **always exceed my limits.**

I played fourteen years in the NFL, and that experience afforded me **many opportunities** for **personal and professional growth, on and off the field.**

When I was young, I was very shy. The role I am in today on TV and radio does not allow me to be shy. Football gave me the **confidence to open up** and **embrace opportunities.** The things I did in football -- **dedication, hard work, research, studying** -- all help me in the career I have today. I have to be **dedicated** and I have to study to know what I am talking about. My growth and commitment to football all throughout the years is an asset in my current career. **The heart of a champion won't be denied, won't quit, and is willing to do whatever it takes to be successful.** My dad said I was a Mitchell and that I could do anything! I stand by those words to this day!

The winning play: Celebrate when you **achieve the dream,** but don't rest. **Challenge** yourself! **Take advantage** of the **opportunities** that are **right for you.**

30
30
M

Fourth Down

Since my retirement from the NFL, I have **worked in the media,** serving as a **broadcaster** and **analyst** for **radio and TV shows.** I am also a champion for **youth in sports,** motivating young people to **work hard, make good life decisions,** and **finish school.**

Comcast
SPORTSNET
Comcast
SPORTSNET

BRIAN MITCHELL
W 1990-1999 W
30
W

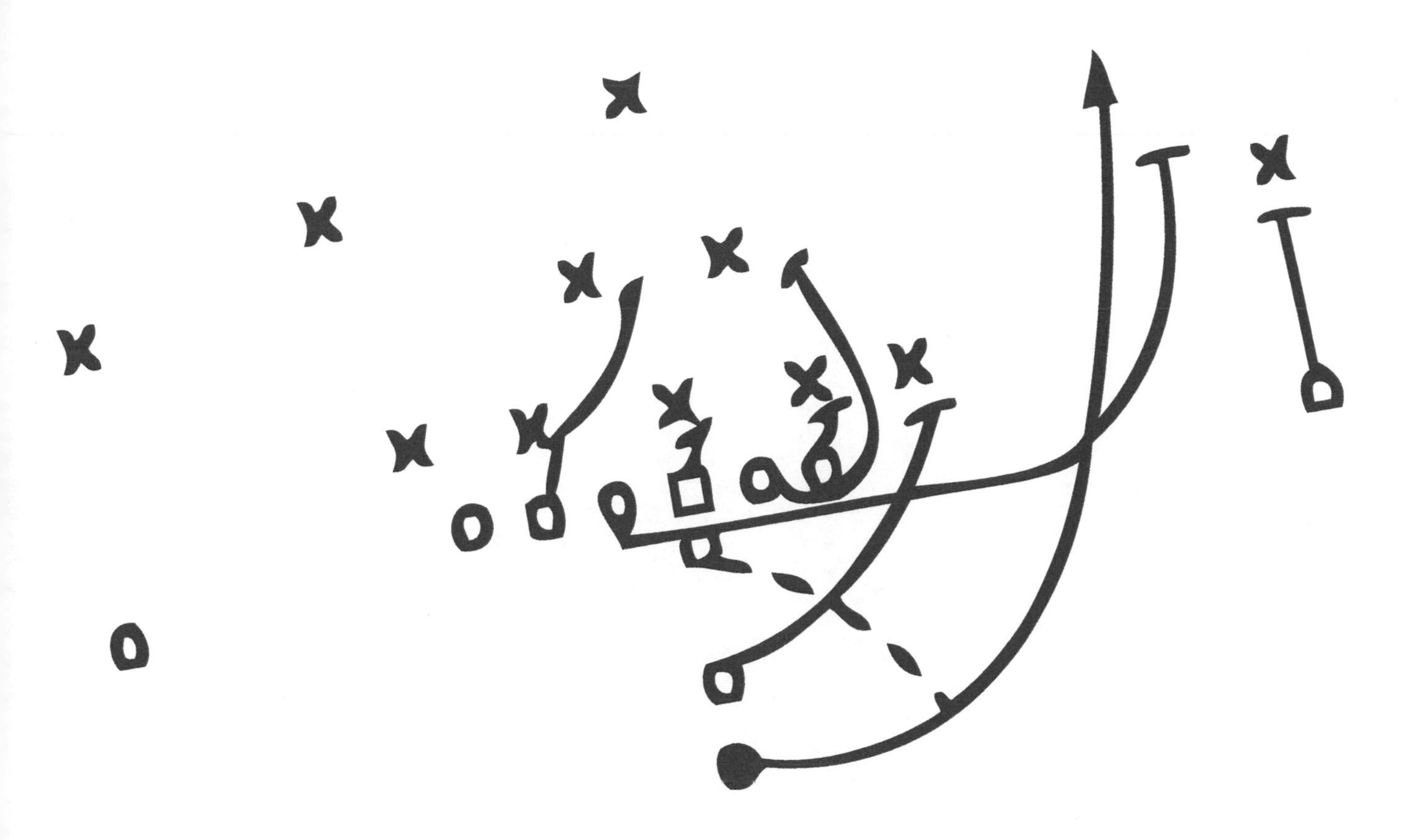

I encourage anyone who dreams of playing in the NFL or in any professional sports league to **never give up! Don't let anyone discourage you from achieving your dream!**

The winning play: If you want the **best out of life,** you must **work hard.** ***There is no shortcut to greatness.***

#astoldbybmitch

Made in the USA
Middletown, DE
03 May 2021